ALTERNATOR
BOOKS™

THE REAL SCIENCE OF
X-RAY AND LASER VISION

Corey Anderson

Lerner Publications ◆ Minneapolis

Lerner Publications Company
An imprint of Lerner Publishing Group, Inc.
241 First Avenue North
Minneapolis, MN 55401 USA

For reading levels and more information, look up this title at www.lernerbooks.com.

Library of Congress Cataloging-in-Publication Data

Names: Anderson, Corey, author.
Title: The real science of X-ray and laser vision / Corey Anderson.
Description: Minneapolis : Lerner Publications, [2022] | Series: The real science of superpowers (Alternator books) | Audience: Ages 8–12 | Audience: Grades 4–6 | Summary: "X-ray and laser vision are handy powers, whether you're a superhero or a scientist. See how scientists use X-rays and lasers to do some amazing things, and find out what the future holds for human vision"— Provided by publisher.
Identifiers: LCCN 2021022453 (print) | LCCN 2021022454 (ebook) | ISBN 9781728441269 (library binding) | ISBN 9781728449616 (paperback) | ISBN 9781728445342 (ebook)
Subjects: LCSH: Medical radiology—Juvenile literature. | LASIK (Eye surgery)—Juvenile literature. | Vision—Juvenile literature. | Superheroes—Juvenile literature.
Classification: LCC R895.5 .A53 2022 (print) | LCC R895.5 (ebook) | DDC 616.07/57—dc23

LC record available at https://lccn.loc.gov/2021022453
LC ebook record available at https://lccn.loc.gov/2021022454

Manufactured in the United States of America
1-49897-49740-7/7/2021

TABLE OF CONTENTS

INTRODUCTION
EYES ON EVERYTHING

Laser vision is a cool but dangerous superpower!

You have been recruited for a very special mission. An hour ago, a huge earthquake shook your city. You have two special superpowers that will help save the day: X-ray vision and laser vision. Rescue workers tell you there are people trapped beneath a collapsed building. You need to move quickly.

You look at the fallen rubble of the building. You activate your X-ray power to see exactly where people are located. They are injured but alive and yelling for help. To save them, you turn on your laser vision to quickly burn a hole in the rubble. Rescuers move in to take the people to safety. You have saved the day!

X-ray vision could help people save lives after earthquakes and other natural disasters.

CHAPTER 1
X-RAYS: A SUPERPOWER!

Real X-ray glasses do not exist—yet!

In comics and movies, X-ray vision is the ability to see through objects. Heroes might be born with this power, or they could have magic items that enhance their vision. They could use this special power to peer through walls and spot criminals. Bank robbers might have X-ray goggles to see exactly what is inside a vault before they break in.

In reality, people don't have X-ray vision. X-rays are a type of powerful, high-energy wavelength of light. Using a special X-ray machine, radiation passes through the less dense parts of the body, like skin and blood. Bones, which are thicker and denser than skin or blood, stop the radiation and show up in X-ray images. Doctors can see broken bones or dense things inside the body that do not belong, such as metal objects.

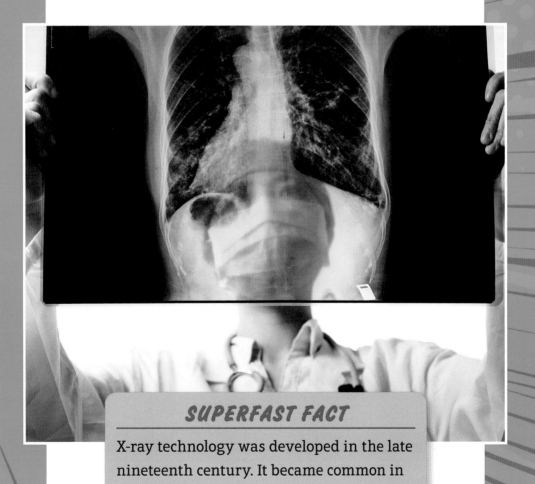

SUPERFAST FACT

X-ray technology was developed in the late nineteenth century. It became common in hospitals in the early twentieth century.

X-rays are used for a similar purpose at airports. Instead of human bodies, they look at luggage. Dual-energy X-ray machines use two X-rays that display what they find on a screen using different colors. Orange indicates that there is organic material present, such as food or plants. Green shows lighter non-organic materials, like soda bottles. Blue means there is metal or heavy plastic present. Using these images, airport security can see if dangerous or illegal things like guns are being carried in someone's luggage.

In movies and TV shows, some heroes cannot see through things lined with lead. Lead is very dense, and it can absorb X-ray waves. It can also help protect us from radiation, which can be damaging to humans and can make us sick. But radiation can also help. Directed X-ray beams can kill cancer cells.

X-ray technology is key to keeping airports safe.

With bulging eyes set on the sides of their heads, chameleons can see in almost any direction.

AMAZING ANIMAL POWER

Prey animals have eyes on both sides of their heads. Their eye position gives them a panoramic view that lets them see forward, backward, and to both sides. This helps them spot predators. Humans, felines, and other predators have eyes that point forward in the same direction. This eye position provides an effect similar to that of X-ray vision. Predators can see through small objects in the foreground and focus on things in the background. This helps them see prey more clearly in cluttered environments like forests.

CHAPTER 2
CUTTING-EDGE LASER VISION

Fictional heroes who have laser vision must be careful when they use their superpower.

Laser vision is another superpower in movies, comics, and TV shows. It lets heroes shoot lasers out of their eyes to destroy walls, dangerous falling objects, or pretty much anything else. This sounds like a very cool ability. But it can be dangerous. What if the power couldn't be controlled?

Sometimes heroes need special equipment to control laser vision. For instance, they might have a visor that blocks their power from shooting out. The visor gives the hero the ability to use the laser vision only when they choose to use it.

Lasers are made up of photons. Photons don't have mass, so lasers don't get hot. Instead, a laser beam cuts through an object by transferring energy to it. The material absorbs the energy and heats up, vaporizing the material where the laser is applied.

Lasers can be powerful enough to cut through diamonds, so cutting through human skin is easy. That's one reason lasers are so dangerous. They can also be used with extreme precision without causing damage to the surrounding areas.

Lasers are so powerful that they can cut cleanly through hard materials.

In action movies, spies often have to climb through complicated laser arrays to avoid setting off alarms. But lasers can also be used by ordinary people for everyday applications. They can mark targets that are far away or make distant objects more visible.

In movies, lasers are often used as visual clues that a security system is protecting something important.

Doctors use lasers to make things visible in a different way. LASIK surgery uses ultraviolet lasers to improve a person's vision. Doctors use a laser to make a small flap in the cornea, which is the surface of the eye. They then lift the flap. Another laser removes tiny tissues from the eye that are causing the vision issues. The flap is put back in place, and the surgery is over. It sounds scary, but it's common surgery that helps many people see better.

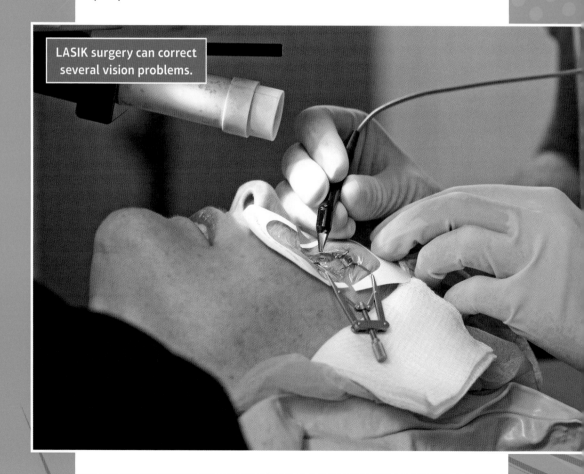

LASIK surgery can correct several vision problems.

Handheld lasers are used in classrooms to point out important information or at home to entertain the family cat. But even seemingly harmless lasers like these come with risks. Used in the wrong way, lasers can harm eyesight by heating the part of the eye that helps us see color.

Handheld lasers are safe as long as they are used correctly.

Green lasers in particular can be damaging to human sight. They have a higher level of radiation. Even low-power lasers can make people feel temporarily blind or cause glare that makes it difficult to see. Think about when you stare at a bright light for too long and then see spots in your vision. Damage from a laser could cause permanent spots. Don't worry though—lasers are fine when used safely and under proper adult supervision.

SUPERFAST FACT

It is illegal to direct a handheld laser at an aircraft. Laser flashes can cause pilots to be temporarily blinded.

CHAPTER 3
SEEING AND SCANNING

Valuable artwork can be X-rayed to make sure it is authentic.

X-ray and laser technologies can help artists. Sometimes, people try to sell fake artwork. They copy a famous painting and claim it is original work. The fakes are so good that even experts are fooled. X-ray technology can also help art dealers see if new art has been painted over an older, less expensive painting.

Over time, old paintings need to be cleaned. It must be done carefully. Cleaning chemicals might damage the paint or the frame. But low-energy lasers can clean paintings safely. Art restorers use lasers in short, controlled bursts to remove impurities.

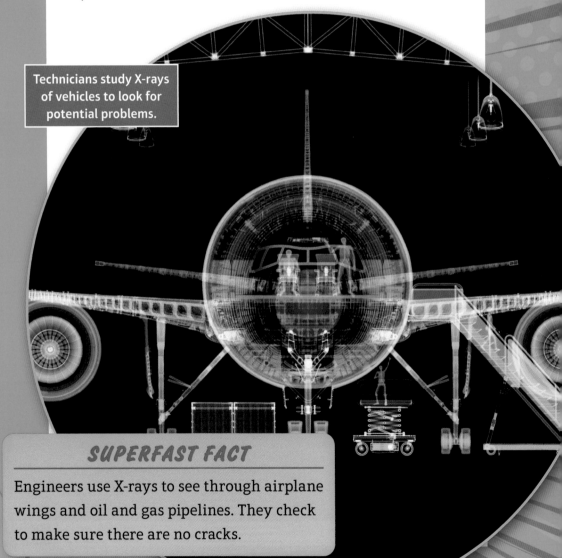

Technicians study X-rays of vehicles to look for potential problems.

SUPERFAST FACT

Engineers use X-rays to see through airplane wings and oil and gas pipelines. They check to make sure there are no cracks.

Archaeologists try to study mummies without damaging them, and X-rays and lasers can help. X-rays can scan the mummy's teeth and bones to determine how old the person was when they died. Lasers take very small, thin samples from the mummy. The samples are tested for different types of elements that tell scientists what life was like in the past.

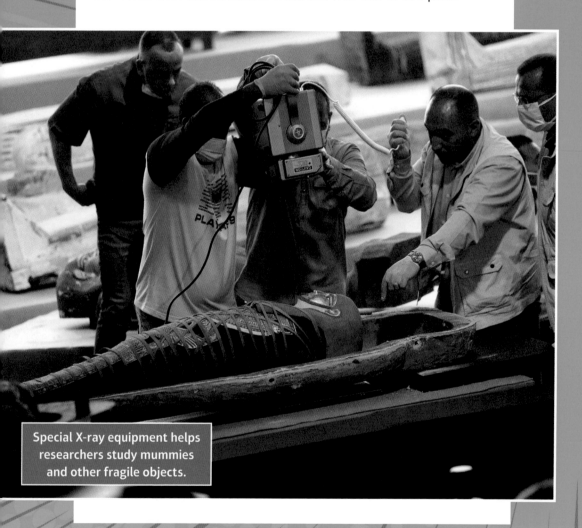

Special X-ray equipment helps researchers study mummies and other fragile objects.

Machines that are about one thousand times more powerful than X-ray machines at hospitals can see dinosaur fossils in great detail. Paleontologists use lasers to detect differences in fossilized animal tissue. The lasers give scientists a better idea of the dinosaur's body shape and color patterns. The lasers can even tell them if the animal had feathers!

A paleontologist examines fossilized bones.

Much of the food we eat is made or packaged in factories. Sometimes, foreign objects, like bits of metal or plastic, end up in food. X-rays scan assembly lines in factories to check for foreign objects. X-rayed food isn't harmful to eat. The amount of radiation that people get from food that has passed through an X-ray machine is very small.

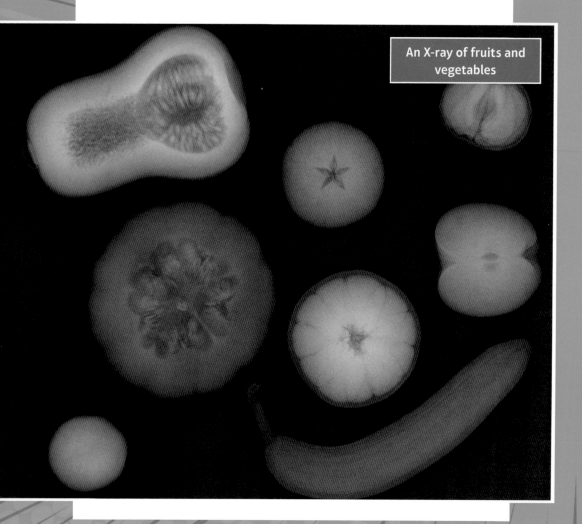

An X-ray of fruits and vegetables

The next time you open a package, take a close look. Some of the pieces were probably cut by a laser.

Lasers are used in food manufacturing too. Laser cutting tools can make quick, clean, and precise cuts for foods like noodles and meat. Lasers do not get dirty or need cleaning like knives do. And they can cut things of different sizes. Lasers also help to make complex food packages and designs to make products more appealing to customers.

CHAPTER 4
X-RAYS AND LASERS OF THE FUTURE

Would you wear contact lenses with lasers inside of them?

Laser vision may be fiction, but laser contact lenses might be part of the future. Scientists are developing a way to add a very thin laser to contact lenses, like a microscopic sticker. It would be powered by light. When activated, the laser would help identify the wearer at security checkpoints.

X-rays are also evolving. A modern X-ray machine sends information to a detector that turns the information into a two-dimensional picture. But our world is three-dimensional. In the future, we may be able to create three-dimensional X-rays that allow doctors to examine body parts from all angles. The machine could scan an injury such as a broken arm from multiple angles, giving doctors a clearer picture of the break. The X-ray would help doctors treat injuries more effectively and diagnose them more accurately.

SUPERFAST FACT

X-ray glasses were first sold around 1909. But people couldn't actually see through things with them. They were just for fun.

It is time-consuming to X-ray every box in a large truck.

X-raying a large area like the inside of a semitrailer is expensive and time-consuming. The whole truck must be unloaded, and each item must be X-rayed in small batches. Scientists are making X-ray machines big enough to scan a whole unloaded trailer at once. Someday, these machines may be common.

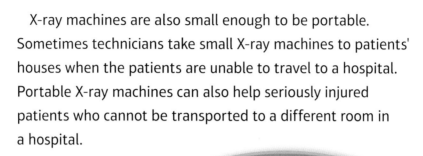

X-ray machines are also small enough to be portable. Sometimes technicians take small X-ray machines to patients' houses when the patients are unable to travel to a hospital. Portable X-ray machines can also help seriously injured patients who cannot be transported to a different room in a hospital.

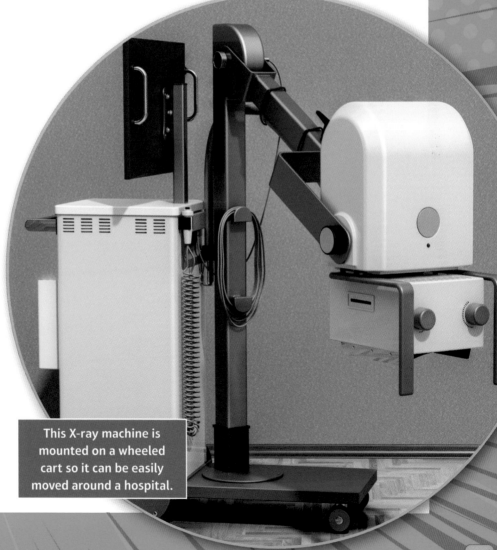

This X-ray machine is mounted on a wheeled cart so it can be easily moved around a hospital.

Lasers are helpful on Earth. But they could be useful in space too! Future astronauts in space might use laser technology to communicate with people on Earth.

Communication between space and Earth relies on radio signals. Radio signals get wider as they travel. That means communicating with someone in a faraway place like Mars requires a gigantic satellite dish to receive the radio signal. Lasers do not diffract, or broaden, as much as radio signals. A much smaller receptor—the size of a pizza—could work as a receiver for laser communication. Scientists are working on this technology. Imagine calling a friend on Mars!

Using lasers, messages could be sent to satellites and then relayed to other parts of the planet or to locations in space.

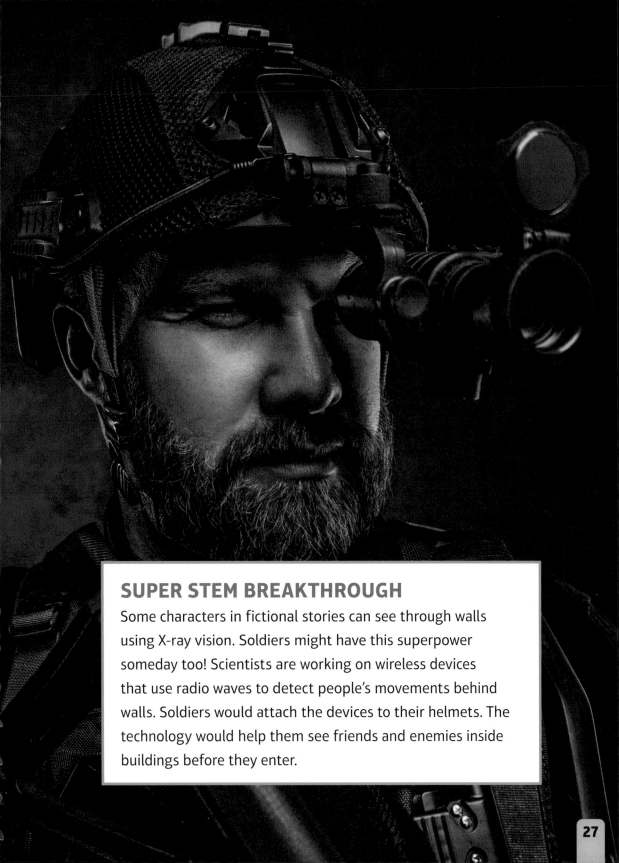

SUPER STEM BREAKTHROUGH

Some characters in fictional stories can see through walls using X-ray vision. Soldiers might have this superpower someday too! Scientists are working on wireless devices that use radio waves to detect people's movements behind walls. Soldiers would attach the devices to their helmets. The technology would help them see friends and enemies inside buildings before they enter.

Special technology can help cars navigate through difficult weather conditions.

Soldiers aren't the only ones who need to see everything. Self-driving cars need to know what's around them to keep their passengers safe. Researchers at Stanford University have invented a device that operates like X-ray vision. This invention helps the cars stay aware of their surroundings in difficult weather conditions, such as fog or heavy rain. In the research lab, the technology can also help cars detect an object on the other side of a foam wall.

X-rays and lasers are incredible technologies that help us live better lives, from saving our lives at hospitals to improving the quality of our food supply. Who knows what other possibilities are yet to come as X-ray and laser technologies continue to evolve!

SUPER YOU!

Grab a friend and play a game of flashlight limbo, pretending the flashlight beam is a laser you have to crawl under. Go into a dark room and have one person point the laser beam a few feet off the ground. The other person has to crawl under the laser beam—just like a spy in a movie—without crossing it. Can you do it?

GLOSSARY

archaeologist: someone who studies remains of past human life and activities, such as jewelry and stone walls

array: a group of elements forming a complete unit

assembly line: a mechanical system used to create products in which work passes from one step to the next

LASIK: a surgical operation that can correct vision problems by removing tissue from eyes with a laser

matter: something that occupies space and has mass

organic: of, relating to, or derived from living organisms

photon: a type of elementary particle

radiation: energy in the form of waves or particles

receptor: a device that senses changes in light, temperature, and pressure

ultraviolet: a form of radiation that is present in sunlight

LEARN MORE

Andrews, John. *Bots and Bods.* Kansas City: Andrews McMeel Publishing, 2021.

Britannica Kids: X-rays
https://kids.britannica.com/kids/article/X-rays/353941

Horstschafer, Felicitas. *X-Ray Me!: Look Inside Your Body.* New York: Greenwillow Books, an imprint of HarperCollins Publishers, 2019.

How Do X-rays See Inside You?
https://theconversation.com/curious-kids-how-do-x-rays-see-inside-you-85895

Kuromiya, Jun. *The Future of Communication.* Minneapolis: Lerner Publications, 2021.

Laser Facts for Kids
https://kids.kiddle.co/Laser

Lord, Michelle. *Patricia's Vision: The Doctor Who Saved Sight.* New York: Sterling Publishing Co., Inc., 2020.

NASA: What Is a Laser?
https://spaceplace.nasa.gov/laser/en/

INDEX

Photo Acknowledgments

Image credits: Mikhail Azarov/Getty Images, p.4; Brasil2/Getty Images, p.5; skynesher/Getty Images, p.6; PansLaos/Getty Images, p.7; MediaProduction/Getty Images, p.8; Reinhard Mink/Getty Images, p.9; alashi/Getty Images, p.10; Pramote Polyamate/EyeEm/Getty Images, p.11; Donald Iain Smith/Getty Images, p.12; DavidKevitch/Getty Images, p.13; Dusan Stankovic/Getty Images, p.14; mikeinlondon/Getty Images, p.15; Hamza Khan/Alamy, p.16; NICK VEASEY/SCIENCE PHOTO LIBRARY/Getty Images, p.17; Ahmed Gomaa/Xinhua News Agenc/Newscom, p.18; Daniel LeClair / Stringer/Getty Images, p.19; Xenia Cobb/Alamy, p.20; john_99/Getty Images, p.21; Jay_Zynism/Getty Images, p.22; DatBot/Wikimedia, 23; BIG_TAU/Getty Images, p.24; AlexLMX/Getty Images, p.25; Steven Puetzer/Getty Images, p.26; FXQuadro/Getty Images, p.27; Kristoffer Tripplaar/Alamy, p.28; nikkytok/Getty Images, p.29;

Cover: Paper Boat Creative/Getty Images